PoetrXY

PoetrXY

For Men Who Don't Read Poetry

JORY COMO

RESOURCE *Publications* • Eugene, Oregon

POETRXY
For Men Who Don't Read Poetry

Copyright © 2026 Jory Como. All rights reserved. Except for brief quotations in critical publications or reviews, no part of this book may be reproduced in any manner without prior written permission from the publisher. Write: Permissions, Wipf and Stock Publishers, 199 W. 8th Ave., Suite 3, Eugene, OR 97401.

Resource Publications
An Imprint of Wipf and Stock Publishers
199 W. 8th Ave., Suite 3
Eugene, OR 97401

www.wipfandstock.com

PAPERBACK ISBN: 979-8-3852-6826-9
HARDCOVER ISBN: 979-8-3852-6827-6
EBOOK ISBN: 979-8-3852-6828-3

01/06/26

CONTENTS

The Family Poet | 1
Starling | 3
Scribbled | 4
Letters | 6
Runaway Daisy | 7
Crestfallen Among Angels | 8
Gethsemane | 10
Gehenna's Revolt | 11
The Immovable Ladder | 12
The Miner | 13
Stuck | 14
Bedside Manners | 17
Under Sabers | 18
Bomb Savant | 20
On Christmas Watch | 21
To Valhalla | 23
A Soldier's Soliloquy | 25
Dissonance | 27
Aveline's Sestina | 28
The Salesman | 30
By Royal Decree | 31
God's Gift | 32
Snow Day | 33
Lucidly | 35
Christmas Party Hop | 36
On Identity | 38
Absent, I | 40

Contents

Avast, Love! | 41
Wilted | 42
Summer's Elegy | 44
Apple Villanelle | 45
Conquered | 46
Defiance | 47
Untitled | 48
The Shat | 49
X Resonance | 50
The Nature of Suffering | 52
Dropping the Ball | 54
The Wager—Part I: The Flop | 55
The Wager—Part II: The Turn | 57
The Wager—Part III: The River | 60
Fireflies | 62
The Bee | 64
The Boomer | 65
Dear Me | 66
The Superfluous | 67
Crescendo | 69
Acclaimed | 72

THE FAMILY POET

It was tough growing up
as the family *Poet*—
our family crest was just a
poem about family crests.

Originally, our surname was French—
La Petite is how it was said,
but we were neither small
nor from France.

We became anglicized
in an emigration accident,
where at the port of entry
we lost a few consonants.
I've read that it was due
to my grandfather's poor
penmanship (or sportsmanship).

My grandmother said after
the renaming they were ecstatic—
finally allowed to stop stooping
and faking French accents.
Now our surname fits,
as my luck would have it.

Genetics revealed that I'm
Norwegian and English.
So I flew the flag of Norway—
until some guy said it was racist.
I guess that flag does look
a bit Confederate.

Let me restart:
My name is Jory,
and I'm an American poet.
I hope you enjoy this eclectic
assortment.

STARLING

Starling, darling, sweet and strong,
whose song were you singing when I came along?
With a confident reply, she made known:
"I was singing a song all my own."

"Lonesome traveler, why have you come?"
Her query alluding to nightfall's doom.
Soaring free over sea toward sunset's step,
as the tide beside her footprints swept.

Captive there on sandalwood shores,
held enchanted by newfound starling lore.
Iridescent, pleasant, kind, and wise—
her—my determined, learned, inspiring muse.

Starling, darling, young lovely one,
effervescently beckoning morning's dawn:
In cadence, your curious song resounding,
admirers beneath your perch, astounding.

SCRIBBLED

You sophisticate me, confessed the indigo ink,
in cursive sprawling elusively across the margins
of page thirteen.

A message to the author, I believed,
reading further on Watts' treatise of
the nature of being and transcendental things—
until reaching page sixteen.

You sophisticate me? In cursive again,
with that blue-purple pen!
This time, a question where the statement had been.

"How?" I replied, setting rationality aside,
half expecting an answer but receiving no chide.
I waited long—then continued on.

I reached the book's end with no other notes from my friend,
pondering what she had meant—I surmised her a woman,
as the penmanship was elegant.

Then I thought a thought:
sophisticate is rarely a verb, a synonym for *complicate*,
really an odd type of word to be used as a compliment.

I reread *The Book* once and then twice,
then a few more times,
sleuthing for clues as to why she scribbled inside
and sophisticated my mind—
sophisticated my simple mind.

LETTERS

If I had 26 letters to trade,
I would keep just 7
to craft you a simple phrase.

So, try words—
say something.
Soft words
are hardly spoken,
Love.

If you replied in a script
that I couldn't read,
I'd travel the world
until I spoke it fluently—

Je t'aime,
te amo,
Ich liebe dich,
    I love you, too.

RUNAWAY DAISY

Mother, your face is red.
Was it something I said, or just the sun?
Mother, they're only friends,
pardon your inquisition.

Don't take back your gifts.
Angry Daisy—you lovely lunatic.
Little sister, don't hide your face.
You don't have to run away.
Don't take back your gifts.
A bindle, Daisy? Such a lunatic.
Little sister, don't pack your bag.
Promise you'll be back someday soon?

Father works so hard
to bring home food for the family.
Treat yourself to a sour mood,
seasoned with apathy.

Don't take back your gifts.
Wrong way, Daisy—you lovely lunatic.
Little sister, don't hide in shame.
You don't have to run away.
Don't take back your gifts,
Daisy Snickelfritz.
Go on and pack your bag,
I promise I'll be back someday for you.

CRESTFALLEN AMONG ANGELS

There was a man who lost his way
and found himself alone one night—
alone, in the abode of mystic fright.
The harvest moon gleamed radiantly,
but through the thick came little light.

His path traversed a winding hollow,
where howling winds and wraiths devised.
Once a shadow seemed to fall—
which did not belong to him at all.
It made him jump, then let a sigh:

"Just a gust among the brambles."

But this was no mundane night.
And though an amber lamplight streamed,
beyond the wick fell little light.

Twice, then again, he startled and shook—
accursed by the way a spooked mind lies.
And fearing grim and ghastly deeds,
he trembled at the wind-stoked phantom's cry.

"Much too old, and much too wise,
to be taken in by such a surprise."

As lifetimes passed, the man grew weary.
Then stumbling aft, he lost his might.
Once more that shadow seemed to stall,
and crawling close, he heard it call.
Tumbling faster towards demise,
his tormented soul gave up the fight.

Reconciled, he dried his eyes:
"Quite a coward, for such a fright."

But proudest day had bowed to night,
where beneath a sullen morning mist,
wayward angels mourn the light.

GETHSEMANE

This world is ending, and I along with it—
my childish dreams, naïve, are upended.
For my children's sake, I petition continuance:
Thirty more years would have been sufficient.

Yet, I find no deliverance.

My anxieties muted, upholding the pretense
that heaven is fair and life is indefinite.
While others pretend and wallow in ignorance,
in hushed tones, we discuss what is imminent.

Still, I find no deliverance.

Before, terrible fates were suffered by others:
When tragedy struck, it was all distant rumor.
Now we are found out—half asleep, unprepared—
an assorted calamity is befalling us here!

This world is ending, and us along with it.

Pray. Pray for our deliverance.

GEHENNA'S REVOLT

Of all the evils man has endeavored,
one yet remains, too long endured.
Convicting mortal nature—a *devil*
masquerades as both magistrate and Lord.

So, in coalition and common reason
the damned then to the depths resort:
where, in concert as resounding Legion,
against the deity they lead revolt.

Together, harmonic in agreement,
the demonic chamber forever pleads.
While the Archon stokes over Hades' ember,
devouring sacraments of ill-will and misdeed.

The guilt it savors is of remorseful flavor—
morsels from the bitter treasure hoard.
Until again, at vengeance end,
the unrepentant feed their god once more.

THE IMMOVABLE LADDER

Up atop a ledge of plaster, rests a pontiff's aging ladder—
remnant of minor renovations finished centuries ago.
Wishing never to encourage the head Cardinal's dreadful dirge—
fearing both whip and scourge—the ladder is left alone.

Set beneath a lancet alcove, sheltering a latticed window,
there, the blessed vestige tempts escape from the holiest abode.
Crafted by a faithful Byzantine, orphaned on an ancient mezzanine—
its Lebanese cedar rails grafting slowly to the stone.

Firmly stayed by a sultan's firman, to assuage Christian clergymen—
whose communal creed prohibits greed so nothing may be owned.
Seven sects there domiciling—indecision their reviling—
each afraid of defiling the holiest of domes.

As a relic, not so haughty—barely five rungs, less than lofty—
leading to a cornice where Armenian gardens once had grown.
Careful not to break tradition, which would up-stoke their division,
priests forewarn perdition if the ladder is ever stowed.

Its prodigious presence lingers outside the Sepulchre's chambers,
testifying to the fractured faith that dogged ladder exposed.
There, a cherished and weathered shrine—in dividing, became less
    divine—
where, too, young men were crucified
        to uphold a Status Quo.

THE MINER

My expertise is coal and soil—
I'm an oracle in the scents of earthen toil.
Everything here is black and cold.
I was once awash in yellowish gold.

As a child, I dreamed of clever escape,
but we miners live out our lives in a cave.
My gaze fixed on latches affixing the gate.
All eyes are on me, as I breathe, and they wait.

Freedom is flitting, far out of reach.
Still, I thrash about—I rage and I preach:
"*Retreat, retreat!*" to men fighting sleep.
Beneath my gilded cage widows weep.

STUCK

A needlestick.

Stifling panic, I freeze to collect myself.
A pulsing strobe of UV light disinfects my memory
as I try to recall my patient's morbidities.

I scrub for a full fifteen minutes—
my patient oblivious,
simply believing that I suffer from OCD.

Hepatitis?

I see glints of their hepatic panel
out of sorts in my mind's eye.
Was their *AST* or *ALT* high?

I. Might. Die.

I should be fine if they have hep B,
my titer promised strong immunity.
But what if they have *hep C?*

. Nice, no track marks that I can see.

What if they have *HIV?!*
I begin my judgmental assessment,
searching for clues in their fit,
questioning their sexuality like it's 1996.

Come off it!

I chide myself.
AIDS is no longer a death sentence,
just look at Magic Johnson—
indeed, his name is a testament.

A subtle chuckle slips.

"Is everything alright?" I'm quizzed,
my patient's patience wearing thin.

"I'm sorry. We had a needlestick,"
I confess.
Impatiently, the man begins to dress
in utter silence.

I ask him to sit,
so I can call the Occ Health nurse,
who loses it,
because her day is now hijacked
by my "incident."

My patient levels an accusation:
"Well, I just hope you're not a gay man."

Confused, I soon realize that he
thinks that I stuck him!
I explain that *I* am the needle's victim,
and it's *his* blood we will be testing.

After my fifteen minutes of washing had ended,
I thawed—and in deep reflection—
pondered how two modern men
were so quick to involve
people who had nothing to do with this.

BEDSIDE MANNERS

My GP is mean.
She tells me I'm fat.
I describe what I eat,
she steals my salt.

In a thick Slavic accent,
she says I'm "*too lah-zee*"
and need to walk more
if I hope to reach sixty.

If I practiced medicine,
I would be much more kind.
Unfortunately, all
my happy patients
would die.

UNDER SABERS

I. You bring me to my knees, let me say I adore you.
If you would—marry me? Even though I just met you.
No, I don't have much money, but my love is true.
If you would marry me, I would promise to adore you.

> I talked with your father, shared my respect for his daughter.
> Asked the man for his blessing and shook his hand when I got it.
> Then I made him a promise and took an oath that was solemn, when I pledged on my honor that I would make you my goddess.

II. Our friends might say we're crazy, so they're not invited.
And if the priest is busy, then he's uninvited.
Because tomorrow I am going away, yet this moment is true.
Consider my love prayerfully. Would you say I do—if I do?

> Once my tour is over and I'm all done playing soldier
> I'll carry you through the doorway of a new home that has got all that old
> white picket fence, and a large yard for our kids,
> where we'll raise up the flag and teach them how to respect.

Wheels up tomorrow, departure at noon.
My ruck is packed with a picture of you.
Under sabers in the sand I stand by, my love,
with a justice of the peace in my issued dress blues.
If you will take my hand, I'll walk with you all the days that I have...

III. *My Dear Soldier,*
> *You don't need a fancy ring to show that you love me.*
> *The diamond sits crookedly—I think that it's lovely.*
> *And when you go away, just leave me two things:*
> *A promise that you'll return soon, and your last name—*
> *because I do.*

From this day forward, for better, for worse
> C-130 rolling down the strip
Forsaking all others and putting you first
> With my main right by my side
To have and to hold till death do us part
> Stand up, hook up, shuffle to the door
In sickness and health, for richer, for poorer
> Jump right out and count to four.

BOMB SAVANT

Another daisy chain is about to blow again.
What's your name, Mr. Trigger Man?

Why you mad, Sergeant Major?
It's just a Ranger-rolled hat, Sergeant Major.
Is that your role here—to protect my clothes from danger?

Ooh, you done it now, young private!
Just get down, young private,
and push the ground—until I'm tired!

These long deployments are bringing me down.
All the way, to where marauders lie.
Avoid the water. Watch that shoulder.

Our old ordinance is bringing empires down.
Lie in wait for the kuffar to pass me by.
Attach the wire. Click the trigger.

ON CHRISTMAS WATCH

The night was still as he gazed across the landscape.
A light fog hung in the air with each breath—
the only company he hoped for this Christmas Eve.
Like a familiar guest being received at the party,
each listless breath slowly dispersed
as another arrived in its place.

The young soldier's eyes traversed slowly,
steadily surveying the bleak terrain.
In the distance, he spotted a small child
taking refuge under a tree,
playing peacefully with a doll.

A welcome sight.

The blackness of the night began to ease,
as blue and green lights adorning the small
yet proud pine illuminated the horizon.
The child played alone,
but was content in his solitude.

The orange glow of a small fire
flickered brilliantly off the tinsel,
dancing gleefully along a shroud of
warmth surrounding the boy.

A soft breeze passed through heavy boughs,
carrying scents of freshly baked ham
and apple pie towards the tower.
The soldier inhaled deeply,
savoring the aroma.

Beyond the berm, he could hear
the faint ringing of bells.
Gradually, the bells faded into joyful voices,
carrying familiar carols from afar.
The chorus was pleasant, but distracting.

This was his final watch,
and his focus was on the boy.
Would he be all right?
The young soldier squinted intensely,
trying to bring his weary vision into focus.

The child animated the small soldier's limbs,
testing the agility of his new gift.
He could see that the child loved the soldier,
and beamed when he hugged it tightly.
The soldier loved the child, too.

And as quickly as his breath dissipated,
the night was still once more.

TO VALHALLA

Wake up.
What have I done?
How could I be so far away from home?
    This feeling,
        I must digest.
No time to get over this right now.
In this cancer, I feel sickness—
is it weakness, or am I just given to this?
    Ashes,
        as we all fall down.
Will the children pick up the pieces?

I don't know how we can live this way,
as fodder for the flames
that flit and flicker, then fade away—
    to Valhalla!

My enemy perplexes me.
We fight because we are sure that we're right.
    And the cowards?
    Not the fallen men.
Shame to those who refuse to stand.

I don't know how I can live this way.
A part of me pleads to stay
in a world that has turned us away—
    to Valhalla!

Then all I feel is nothing,
    and all I want is morphine—
        please just give me something to get me out of my head!

And all I need is one thing:
    To know if you'll still love me.
Will you see me through this dread?

My heart is beating so fast—I don't know how long I'll last.
    Bullets all around now,
I hear them cracking as they pass.

Am I a stranger to the angel?
    Queen of Battle—djinn or angel!

I see that I will not last the day;
Valkyries have spoken my name.
Rage, as the light begins to fade—
    to Valhalla!

My heart is beating so fast—I don't know how long I'll last.
Bullets all around now—
    I feel the plates crack in my vest.

A SOLDIER'S SOLILOQUY

Who let him waste his time?
Who lit his soul on fire?
Why'd you tell him he's wanted for murder?
It's not a selfish crime.
He signed on the line.
Why'd you say you'd support him forever?

Stay away from this fight,
unless you're truly on our side.
Have we forgotten what is right?
Issue us grace,
truth,
and light.

So little precious time.
We're at the contact line.
Why don't you come down and lead us!?
I've read the battle plans.
I don't like how they end.
If we've reached the end, come and relieve us.

Finally, I see—
for the first time clearly—*that I can't see!*
Now I believe that inside my head
there's only me.

With all this empty silence,
all that I ask is: *Why?*
Why'd you say that we're wanted for murder?
Now all these thoughts are through me—
I have no alibi.
Why'd you say you'd sustain us forever?

Stay away from this life,
unless you're truly on our side.
Fleeing outposts in the night—
overrun,
abandoned
in a hopeless fight.

Come teach me wrong from right
and I promise
I'll lead a peaceful life.
Bearing a guidon for the light,
with mended wings,
I'll trace the sky.

DISSONANCE

We served our time with honor and pride,
yet the purpose of it eludes me.
For what prize did we detonate our minds
into fragments over trash-laden wadis?

"For the right to vote!" the fools deluded—
congratulating elected oppressors.
Then, upon returning home, we found ours
a sodomized and disfigured culture.

Where were the warrior feminists at,
with their proud velveteen vagina hats,
when Yazidi girls were taken and bound?
They were found in performance of curtsy and bow,
before men in wigs and talcum.

Perhaps the youth would return us to sanity,
inspired by tales of a former glory?
Impossible—the whole next generation raised
sanctimoniously, on race guilt and self-loathing.

So, we end on the refrain, "Goddamn the USA!"
as wild children burn cities to the ground.
Let them eat cinder, each other, and cake,
while the dissidents take a knee this round.

AVELINE'S SESTINA

If you live, I'll teach you to swim—
I promise, my love, please don't die.
Fight to stay in for five more days.
Your mother is determined, strong,
and they are sending us back home
until she is further along.

I wish that I had gone along
when your mother went for that swim
in the spring at our new lake home,
where she had nightmares you would die.
She bled, and the current was strong
that night—continuing for days.

At twenty-two weeks, zero days,
they said you weren't enough along
to survive and your lungs weren't strong,
because without water to swim
and breathe in, you would surely die.
So, for days we waited at home.

On day five we left our new home,
gone now for these forty-two days.
I worry that your mom will die
today when they cut her along
her delicate belly. Please swim
little one, tread, be strong.

Your mother's faith in fate is strong
and her body has been your home—
remember those times you would swim
as one? Her journal knows those days.
Now, I should be moving along,
holding faith that my girls won't die.

But if worse comes, and you do die,
please know—we know that you were strong,
and we have loved you all along.
We will take you back to our home
and visit you on cloudy days,
then in tears, teach you how to swim.

She knew all along if they'd die.
Teach me to swim, my love—your strong
will guides us home to brighter days.

THE SALESMAN

I'm not ready for this.
I'm not ready for this.

Then tear it out,
like a zealous fireman!
Planned future now—
for her, but not for them.

In pieces—a broken person.
Can't feel at all—
      who's inhuman?

You're running scared,
into false saviors.
Tied up? Let our curettes
unchain you.

Fatherless child—
mother's dysplasia.
A pound of cure and
an ounce of aspiration.

BY ROYAL DECREE

Monarchs I would overthrow,
and turrets build row by row,
if only it made it so—
you could be a Princess.

Your mother I would crown Queen;
your brother Prince, and I a King.
Royalty would be our thing—
you would be a Princess.

Daughter, I thee coronate,
name bestow on castle gates.
In tiaras so ornate—
you would be a Princess.

Darling girl, I love you so:
graceful, lovely, beautiful.
I want you to always know
that you are a Princess.

GOD'S GIFT

Theodore, my thoughtful son,
remain true to who you are.
Even when it's unpopular,
have your own opinion.

Take the time to learn when taught.
Make *wonder* your companion.
Ensure your voice is your own.
Ponder all with careful thought.

Fall in love with abandon.
Don't protest a broken heart.
If you ever feel distraught,
remember, you can come home.

Be yourself, my brilliant boy,
as bright as you choose to be.
Brave, sincere, kind, and sweet,
Theodore—*God's gift* to me.

SNOW DAY

"Wake up! Wake up!"
the importunate little clock demands,
as your clumsy hand searches for the snooze button.
The howl of a frigid wind concedes
rare permission to rest a moment longer.

In step, the hypnotic aroma of a freshly
brewed pot beckons the senses.
The auto-start timer on the brewer serves to
remind that technology is a mixed blessing.
Indeed, the clocks are working together
towards your quickening on this winter's morn.

Taunting the wind behind a pane of frosty glass
you attempt to coax the sun out,
offering up a toast with a hand-painted ceramic mug.
Best Parent Ever, it reads,
in squiggly gold fingerpaint.

A little boy drags himself to your side,
blankie in tow.

"Can we stay home today?" he pleads,
rubbing one sleepy eye with the sleeve
of a plaid flannel pajama.

"But what about work and school?" you question,
searching deep for the answer.

In an epiphany, the disheveled little boy exclaims,
"Your work could be to teach me today!"

Surely such an astute child
can afford a day away from school.

Between spoonsful of cinnamon-spiced oatmeal
from a shared kettle,
you learn how to make snickerdoodles—
perfecting the art of burnt bottoms.

The sun arrives late over the treetops,
chasing the nagging wind away
in an apologetic gesture.

A freshly rolled snowman is soon partitioned
into ammunition for an impromptu snowball fight.
Merriment triumphs, as last year's Christmas puppy
bounds after snowballs dissolving into a sea of white.

The large, medium, and small snow angels
remind you of how much your little family has grown—
and how much more it could grow.

"Wake up!" the persistent little clock demands,
with all the haste of a passing dream.

"Wake up and live!"

LUCIDLY

Ah, darkness still,
and I
between dream and real,
grasp her hand as I wake.

From terrors fleeing,
or we, as lovers quarreling,
share nightmare
or turbid state.

Clench my eyes.
Again, worlds fleeting—

then, paradise.

CHRISTMAS PARTY HOP

I didn't *have* to step into the knee-deep snow
to realize that our little car was stuck—
but I did.
A sudden gust tossed fresh powder onto my seat
as I shoved the reluctant door open.

Great, I thought.
Now I'll have wet legs to complement my soaked foot.

Christmas music played gleefully
through the earpiece of my phone
while we waited on hold
for roadside assistance.

Our young son stirred wildly in the back seat,
recounting the story of our spinning and whirling off the road—
with great enthusiasm.
I couldn't recall the *whoosh, boom, blam!*
but the adrenaline was subsiding,
and I was starting to feel the frosty bite
in my snow-filled shoe.

The first car to approach us continued on.
I don't blame them.
Once stopped, small cars barely get enough traction
to take off again.

Slowly, then steadily, the persistent growl
of an old pickup cut through the blustery mire.
A single working taillight lit the icy black asphalt,
as a stalwart 1970-something Ford slid to a sideways stop.
The red glow, coupled with *Let It Snow* crackling
like a vintage vinyl through my phone,
renewed a sense of holiday ambiance.

A bundled figure jumped out of the truck
with hasty determination.
I was amazed as he instinctively dove under our rear bumper—
a well-worn tow strap in hand.
Two tugs later, and we were free of the icy trap.

"You're a lifesaver," I said,
graciously offering a folded twenty.

"No worries," he said,
waving off my payment with a smirk.
"But you should get your bumper fixed."

We exchanged a "Merry Christmas,"
as he left in search of another rescue.

Surveying my bumper,
I found no damage—
simply a faded campaign sticker from yesteryear.

Realizing the jest in his comment, I smiled,
and my heart became a little warmer—
although my foot was still ice cold.

ON IDENTITY

An azure lanyard
around your neck
carries a tiny photo of you,
lest you forget who you are
or where you're at.

It assures others
that you are legit—
identifiable in a
one-inch pic, quite small,
but your smile's big.

The obscure position
in which it sits:
above your navel,
below your chest,
is where it rests best.

It's secured across
the nape of your neck
with a plastic clasp, made
to break fast if tugged
with violence.

You are sure to bring
it with when you leave
for work, except today
when you forgot—dang.

Maybe it's *cyan*?

ABSENT, I

I'm becoming translucent—
it's hardly a gift.
Some light gets let through,
not much stays within.

My words fall shallow,
rarely reaching an ear.
My sounds might echo,
if they knew I was here.

I've consulted a mirror,
who reassures I'm still there—
but predicts opacity
by the end of the year.

So, I guess I'll keep on
whatever this is,
until I am gone
and transparency wins.

AVAST, LOVE!

When did a heart-shaped blockade
    start raining down on your parade?
Would you mean to send me away—
    rock and sway, rock and sway!

If you love me,
then why won't you love me?
Crossing blades to my heart—
    there's a mutiny.
Silk sheets flowing like waves
from our balcony.
Lost thoughts tend to betray
    when they make believe.

You were that lovely mistake
    who still takes my breath away.
Can't you see I'm walking a plank—
    crash or stay, crash or stay!

If you love me,
then why won't you love me?
Truth, I'm crossing my heart—
    there's no make-believe.
A silk flag folding in waves
at our eulogy.
With our backs to the gale,
    we'll sail into eternity.

WILTED

A rose is wilting in front of you—
mind her broken thorns, tread softly.
Shattered, staring back at you,
the petals and broken glass of a white vase.

Breathe it in, then breathe it out.
Take it in, then let it out.
Speak it softly, speak it loud.
Finally, say it all out loud!

Something's different, something's changed.
Nothing really feels the same.
Cinders, ashes, are what remain
of promises we made that day:

To have and to hold, till death do us part—
　I'm dying now!
To honor, to love, for all of our days—
　you're crying now!

I'm still standing in front of you.
Take your foot off the gas—for my sake.
A mirror here shattered in front of you.
Gaze through broken glass to my face.

How did we get so far along this way?
Twisted, wilted, frayed—fully on display?
The solution to dissolution is an illusion—
it's our grand delusion; it's time to move on.

Some things differ, some things change.
Nothing ever stays the same.
Cinders, ashes, are what remain
of promises we made.

Petals falling down—
      all falling down now.
Fall petals fall—
      all falling.

SUMMER'S ELEGY

My embattled, battered constitution:
broken, crumbling bulwarks ever weakened.
Hers, a staunch and bitter opposition.
Love—the victim of capricious seasons.

Summer's cooling fueled a raging tempest,
churning, worsening insecurities.
Never falling, ever flailing—we existed,
wracked against backdrops of a brackish sea.

Quietly we lay, completely shattered.
Our entangled flame had been extinguished.
Where once our love had truly mattered,
I, beside the stone vignette, had perished.

There, in bronze, our fairest youth is captured,
fading—finest hours forever pictured.

APPLE VILLANELLE

All apples are Honeycrisp now,
not as sweet as they were before.
Eventually, they all turn brown.

Fairly common, sold by the pound
in every produce-selling store—
all apples are Honeycrisp now.

Old cultivars are not around;
one rarely finds Braeburn anymore.
Eventually, they all turn brown.

Once, Granny Smith had fed the town
with latticed pies and cidered cores—
all apples are Honeycrisp now.

At first bite, they made quite the sound,
with flesh as crisp as autumn's morn.
Eventually, they all turn brown.

By October, boughs touch the ground,
but no one picks fruit off the floor.
All apples are Honeycrisp now.
Eventually, they all turn brown.

CONQUERED

After "The Conqueror Worm" by Edgar Allan Poe

Oh, how the streets have changed,
passing fast these fourteen years.
A summer's child—anxious, pained—
innocent pallor wears her fears.
Close behind, the tribes encroach,
veiled in their muffled jeers.
Theirs—a fevered, pitch-perfect harmony
to the muezzin's triumphant cheers.

A child, the form of God on high,
whose father's God is laid low—
in betrayal of his daughter by
perfidious puppets who come and go.
Her bid, less than that of foreign kings
to whom her heritage is doled.

And all that once was sovereign lies
broken, bruised, and sold.

DEFIANCE

Tumbling through time,
a mist of loam enshrines
a glimpse of an angel's untimely
demise.

An apparition of Atropos,
cutting her threads shy—
so when plucked, she might choose
to die.

Sworn never to be the unwilling bride
of some dreadful lord. Unwedded—
her dress torn where faithful sisters
stitched wings inside.

In defiance, the goddess throws
herself down onto a bed of nightshade
sewn into the gown.

Loosed, the spool begins to unravel,
until uncoiled—she's freed—
becoming immortal.

UNTITLED

Modern poets, what a miserable lot:
uninspired, grotesque—intent to shock.
Once, authors sought wonder in a lover's kiss.
Now, they seek tenure in descriptions of piss.

In pretentious confessions and joyless musings,
"Insta-poets" sling drivel that dulls one's thinking.
Remember storytelling? Meter? Rhyme?
Or how Whitman inspired with brilliant lines?

Literature today is too partisan, too bland—
a never-ending lecture on "whiteness" and men.
It's true that writing is therapeutic in many regards,
but grievance alone doesn't make one a bard.

Before, great journals inspired and amused
offering novel, thought-provoking views.
Now they peddle lewdness meant to impress
lechers and deviants—the gatekeepers of press.

I concede: this verse isn't brimming with wit.
It's basic—some bullshit that fits.
To be honest, no one cares. Let prosody die.
Then eulogize it using boorish prose
and fragmented
lines.

THE SHAT

There it sat—
the shat.

From a dog,
    from a cat.
Where'd it go?
    I don't know!
Oh shat—
    it's on my shoe
. . .ewww.

X RESONANCE

For those times that defined us,
both shaped and aligned us.
When our words left us fleeting
and what passed was behind us.

When portraits of families
lined brown-paneled hallways,
and family tradition meant
church-school on Sundays.

When on weekdays our
insufferable parents divorced us,
burned down our homes
and abruptly displaced us.

When we raised ourselves
like little adults,
and by the age of fourteen
we were addicted to smoke.

When pop culture shamelessly
tapped into our pain,
and we felt the cathartic
wailing of a man named Cobain—
battered—his Jaguar screaming,
shattered
under intense rage.

That resonates,
    just as deeply today.

THE NATURE OF SUFFERING

Once, I woke in a realm of monsters,
where gentle creatures grazed in the meadow,
while others found meadows wholly inedible.
Denied a peaceful life of ease and wonder,
the latter grew claws and fangs that were dreadful.

That world was divided, its resources hidden.
Its land subject to famine and scarcely provisioned.
We all lived in terror, in fear of predation.
Most died in pain from disease or starvation.

The winters were frigid, yet creatures warm-blooded.
In summer, the forests raged in flames—then were flooded.
Mountains quaked and the seas would rise,
overtaking mothers and young by surprise.

Then clever primates found an advantage.
They developed science, engineering, and medicine.
But the realm was quick to feign a great weakness—
it would never stop inflicting suffering and carnage.

With its secrets uncovered in that brief reprieve,
that sphere changed its temperature by a single degree.
Societies ceased, quickly reverting in time.
Antibiotics stopped working. Then the water ran dry.

If ever you wake in such inhospitable terror,
one fashioned by that artistic sadist called *Nature*,
be quick to enjoy whatever you can,
because you're here—then you're not.

The nightmare of man.

DROPPING THE BALL

All people are assholes now—
their words a lame crescendo.
Most old friends wear partisan frowns,
and humor lacks innuendo.

Every bee is a pissed-off wasp—
true honeybees went extinct here.
There's no more water for the crops.
Every year's hotter than last year.

Men are worthless without money.
Money's nearly worthless too.
Comedians stopped being funny.
Influencers are mostly lonely.

Mom's a prostitute, but her own boss.
Romance is easy: casual.
The standard home's a million bucks.
All drugs are laced with fentanyl.

Hurray! Let us celebrate old times past
and look forward to new memories.
If only I could kick this cough,
and afford some decent groceries.

THE WAGER—PART I: THE FLOP

I was perplexed. Was this win the result of divine intention or mere serendipity? Either way, I was certain I wasn't worthy of such fortune. *My God*, I thought. *What would now be expected of me? And if I failed to meet that expectation, what might be exacted from me?*

I stared blankly at the lottery ticket scanner. "See Lottery Official," it flashed in brilliant digital blue. On any other day, I would've stifled my excitement until confirming the amount beyond the vague promise of that notoriously fickle machine. After all, any win over $599 requires a trip to the state lottery headquarters for confirmation. But recent rumors of a local jackpot win gave me uncharacteristic confidence that I was holding a ticket worth far more than six hundred dollars.

For half a week, the town had been buzzing. Word spread that the winning ticket had been sold at the solitary mom-and-pop shop in our typical Midwestern town. Our quaint, two-pump service station had become the center of the world—or at least the center of the county. It was the state's last true mom-and-pop: short one Mom, with Pop not far behind. Though the garage had been shuttered for years, the store still smelled of new tires and cherry pipe tobacco.

"You alright, son?" a familiar elderly voice called from across the counter. Snapping out of my trance, I wiped the saliva pooling at the edge of my lip.

"Yes, I'm fine, thank you," I replied, gathering myself and heading for the exit. The old brass bell rang out as I crossed the black-and-ivory checkered tile that marked the threshold of the narrow side entry.

Hastily, I retreated to the comfort of my late-model gray sedan—except the seat wasn't familiar, nor was the purse or baby blanket sitting unattended in the passenger seat. A jolt of panic surged through me. *Pump One—you always park at Pump One!*

After years of fidelity, I'd finally been seduced by the siren song of Pump Two.

Panic melted into a novel amusement. *How cool would it be if I shoved this winning ticket into that purse?* A kind of reverse pickpocketing—a *pockpicketing*—one might say. I recalled hearing a story once, in which 1980s comedy hero Bill Murray snatched a handful of fries from a fast-food patron, taunting them with the fact that no one would ever believe them. I wondered if I could get away with such a shenanigan. Possibly. But giving away my only ticket to celebrity felt like a catch-22. So, I balked—quickly fleeing the scene in my own late-model gray sedan.

THE WAGER—PART II: THE TURN

The state lottery offices were unimpressive—more business than casual, more Formica than granite. Not what I expected from the headquarters of a billion-dollar operation. The "greenroom," which was beige, featured framed nature prints of mallards and noble stags, as if serenity justified state-sanctioned gambling. Bureaucracy hung in the air—not just in the decor, but in the officials themselves. Only government could make giving away money feel like a solemn chore.

My anxiety grew as the shuffle of reporters filtered through the thin walls. State law forbids anonymity. The press conference was technically optional, but "highly recommended"—meaning they placed your oversized check center stage and waited for you to claim it.

I chose the cash option, as most do. After taxes, I'd walk away with less than many people retire with, yet I was encouraged to use the phrase "a million" liberally. My dreams of becoming a D-list celebrity began to melt. I wouldn't be getting away with stealing appetizers from unsuspecting restaurant patrons, as Bill Murray once had. As the minute hand crept toward the hour, my mind wandered. I wondered if the state might use its cut of the jackpot to repaint the greenroom something less drab—or at least more green.

Days earlier, before tax math and annuity options had sobered me, my mind had been flooded with self-serving fantasies. I envisioned a mansion—then envisioned dusting it. I imagined its vast many rooms, all void of imagination. Out of habit, I returned to the mom-and-pop shop and bought my weekly ticket. Pop was behind the counter, printing lottery numbers for tomorrow's drawing. It had become our ritual, a small-town perk, I suppose.

For years I'd worked the late shift at the nursing home, often picking my ticket up the morning after the drawing. I'd gotten to know Pop well while caring for Mom before she passed. Maybe it's sentimental, but I liked to pretend that we were something of a family. The elderly couple had no children, but they had a fondness for wayward souls like mine. The many once-stray cats that called the shop home could attest to that. It was Mom's and Pop's encouragement that nudged me toward college after years of ambivalence.

Pop was generous with his wisdom. More than that, he was trustworthy. I hadn't told anyone about my good fortune yet, savoring the last morning of my anonymous, fiscally challenged existence.

"Pop?" I asked. "What would you do if you prayed for a million dollars and the prayer was answered?" He smirked, retrieving an older preprinted ticket from the drawer beneath the till.

"I wouldn't pray for such a blessing," he said. "I'd pray that I got to be the blessing of someone else's prayer."

His voice carried the weight of nine decades—and probably a few pounds of cherry pipe tobacco. I took a moment to absorb it, fishing through my pockets for the last four quarters I'd found stuck to an old gum wad in the cupholder of my sedan.

"Keep your dollar, son," he said, tossing the old ticket into the trash beneath the counter. "The ticket is no good *this time*," he added with a grandfatherly wink.

He knew! He must have watched the ten o'clock news when the numbers were drawn. He knew the ticket from days earlier had been a winner, and still he had sold it to me after the fact for a dollar.

I nodded and murmured a soft, sincere "thank you." What else could I say? I sauntered out through the narrow doorway, knowing I wasn't deserving of the fortune I'd soon be claiming.

Back in the beige present, a woman with sleek graying hair—pulled back as tightly as the grip she kept on her clipboard—peeked through the door of the beige greenroom and asked if I was ready. I glanced over my notes one last time and followed her to the stage.

Cameras clicked in rapid succession as I stepped into the strobing spotlight. Before I even spoke, the fanfare faded. I wasn't the object of a paparazzi frenzy—just the passing interest of a dozen local reporters seated in cheap, state-owned folding chairs. Half were scrolling their phones; the other half made small talk.

An overweight man towards the back began packing up his camera, having already captured my dumbfounded face. I began to suspect I'd overestimated the public's interest in watching an ordinary guy receive a six-digit check—regardless of its industrial poster-board and glitter-paint composition.

I paused, inhaled, and gripped the podium with both hands, steadying myself against the weight of the moment. From the inner breast pocket of my worn tan coat, I drew a thin bifold wallet. Inside, folded like a secret, was a torn page from a spiral notebook. As I opened it, flecks of paper—confetti from the jagged edge—drifted to the floor. I slipped the wallet back into my coat, my knuckles grazing my chest. My heart thudded like a drum in a quiet room.

I'd always loved writing my little soliloquies. Performing them, though—that was another matter. But this was the moment I had asked for. And the place where I had asked it from made all the difference. The courage to proceed came from the familiarity that diligent rehearsal had intended.

And so, I made my wager:

THE WAGER—PART III: THE RIVER

"It is by chance—and perhaps by grace—that we are all here today. After much contemplation, I've decided to give this money away. And I'm asking for your help.

"When you donate to a worthy cause, I will match your gift until the prize money is gone.

"The stipulations are few.

"First, let's not make this political. Charity that deepens division is no charity at all. And if our giving is merely self-serving, is it truly altruism?

"Second, please give from the heart. Step outside the comfort of anonymity and into the vulnerability of community. Let your light shine. Some will say we should give in secret, to store up treasure in heaven. But what then of that treasure? If we forfeit a portion to the tax of ego yet invest it in the quickening of the human spirit—perhaps that's a trade worth making.

"Third, give creatively. Give beyond what you've given before. Use this moment to inspire. Develop your gifts. Money is only one form of currency. If you meet someone new, you may already have what they need—or they may help you fill a need you didn't know you had.

"So, I ask you to go this mile with me. Could you go two?

"I'm not so naïve as to think all the world's problems can be solved with a little money on a big check. But a million people inspiring millions more would change the world. Perhaps, after our money is spent, the world will reflect on this cause as one of foolish hope. But then again—the world will reflect. And if history is to record us as fools, let it record our folly as one composed of faith, love, and radical goodwill.

"I know even a little time or money is a lot to ask. Just last week, twenty dollars—or even twenty minutes—felt like a sacrifice. It took a great amount of wealth for me to realize that wealth isn't measured by what we have, but by what we do with it.

"And if all we purchase with our audacious charity is the sentiment that people on this side of the planet gave up a fortune so that a hungry family a world away could dine together for an evening—then the cost was worth the price of the plate.

"Please join me. Invest in each other with sincere personal affection, and I will meet you there. Ask, and you shall receive—so long as you ask in love and faith. Ask, and it will be given to you.

"Ponder that for a moment. But ponder it with this revelation: the speech you're hearing today was written three years ago, long before my numbers were drawn—crafted as entertainment for a dear, grandmotherly store clerk who encouraged me to always be prepared for an answered prayer.

"I hope you're as excited as I am to begin this adventure. I'm not simply giving this money away—I'm inviting you to invest with me in the hope of our shared posterity. A million dollars could be just the beginning. How high could we take it? I believe—much higher."

* * *

In the weeks that followed, hundreds—then thousands—joined the cause. We crowdfunded a revolutionary yet simple idea: that together, we were everything any of us needed.

Pop and I watched in amazement as the message of reckless altruism spread like wildfire. Maybe people were drawn by the promise of matched donations. Maybe they just wanted to see if an ordinary person would really give away a lottery jackpot.

Whatever the reason, people gave—time, talent, kindness—and it mattered. No hospitals were built, but many were healed. No lasting organizations were formed, but for a season we came together.

I came to understand that the money was never really mine to spend as I pleased, yet I had been blessed to do just that.

Through giving ourselves away, we became free.

And just as I wagered, the world did reflect—and in our reflection, we saw something beautiful.

FIREFLIES

Olly, olly, oxen free—
all the kids would say
under the willow trees
where we carved our names.

Built a rocket ship,
on the top is where we'd sit.
Where we stole a beer from your dad—
but we each just took one sip.
We were such good kids.
Look how we got to live.
Riding, smoking, joking—
the prince and princess of '96.

Olly, olly, oxen free—
all the kids still say
under the willow trees
where we carved our names.

Dog days at the lake.
Water fights at the parade.
Fireworks displayed
over hills where we would lay.
There's so much I could say
about the way the world would change
if we only knew—
summers end too soon.

But I would still kick the can with you,
catch some fireflies,
then set them loose
under shooting stars
where I wished I was your dude.
Then you kissed me first
and made that wish come true.

THE BEE

Once I heard a bumbling bee
stuck inside a canopy—
startled, I sought to set him free,
but instead I found a wasp.

Stomping wild—instinctively—
I forgot that I had worn bare feet
and was therefore stung immediately,
leaving me to ponder:

Why did he behave so aggressively?

THE BOOMER

The weather's changing,
I feel it in my bones.
>*That gun went off too close to my head!*
New floral arrangements,
my name marked in stone.
>*That gun went off too close to my head!*
Share your story, young American—
>*don't you know that I've fought in two wars?*
They tried to lock me up,
but I'm built like stone.
>*Don't you know that I've fought in two wars?*

It feels like rain today.

DEAR ME

It's Tuesday night and I'm not feeling quite right,
not bad, per se. Am I dead or alive?
Then I begin to wonder: *What's the point of this?*
Pacing around the escape room, stumbling over clues I've missed.

We narrate our lives in auto-erotic biographies,
wasting all our time gyrating on little screens.

Don't try—just shrug and sigh.
"Get out of me," said the flower to the bee.
Oh me, oh my. Let loose, then hang tight.

Dear me, goodbye.

Hang on—the lock opens from inside.

THE SUPERFLUOUS

It was not meant to be—the snowflake,
performing pirouettes gracefully.
Its presence was unexpected.
Such inclement weather was rare:
snow falling on Easter Sunday?
The mass was scandalized; the Father, underprepared.
Still, I waited impatiently—already ushered.

The congregation had planned for a pleasant resurrection.
The mass was to be held beneath an old oak tree.
Its timbers would serve as a solemn reflection—
a spring morning, the backdrop for a
poignant Easter message: *Life renewed!*

No one had prepared for the frigid Christmas vestige.

A trembling widow stirred from her pew,
gently kneeling in genuflection.
She searched far beyond the window,
finding the timid flake below the steeple—
contemplating purpose and direction.

With calloused hands clenched in prayer,
the dear woman repeated a worn petition.
A wayward breeze, in search of solace,
carried the orphan towards a sterling chalice,
where it received the sacrament of Holy Baptism.

At the conclusion of mass, we shared in the Doxology.
There, in solemn reflection, I thanked circumstance
for open windows, young mothers,
persistent widows—and all others—
who, like me,
were never meant to be.

CRESCENDO

Faint against competing twilight, where the skylines fade to midnight—
hung amidst a backlit canvas still expanding from its core.
Asteroids wove between the seven noble rings of Saturn,
fast encroached upon the vastness separating Earth and Star.
Much we marveled their majestic arrival from beyond the stars.

Mostly we felt trepidation, mixed with guarded celebration,
as the news of newfound comets gradually traveled near and far.
Men debated, trading comments: "How to class and name the objects?"
Some said asteroid, others comet; children preferred *shooting star*.
Like a child, I was beguiled into setting my wish upon the stars.

First among them was Apollyon, aptly called *Lord of Destruction*.
Easily, he was the largest—in diameter a hundred yards.
More maligned than all the others, further outcast than his brothers—
King of bright and splendid colors—boldly leading as royal vanguard.
Though it was his younger brother whom the people most adored.

Second-born was Prince Crescendo, best known by his resplendent glow.
Dubbed by some *The Smooth Criminal,* for shining like a diamond glove.
Made up more of ice than metal—one part iron, two parts nickel—
in orbit unpredictable and difficult to know.

Given their close proximity, we expected quite a show.

Finally, trails of light appeared between the moon and exosphere.
Strangely, though, they changed in bearing—summoned by a mischievous force.
Soon I grew to anxious fearing, as the glowing asteroids nearing—
straying, waving, wildly veering—quickly left their charted course.
Such an unexpected shift had left mankind without recourse.

As their close approach proceeded, tides along the shores retreated,
fast revealing parts of nature, much better left there undisturbed.
Men of good repute and stature, desperate for impending rapture,
realized only mad disaster: all rapacious urges purged.
Men of faith, in losing faith, no longer sought their sins obscured.

Witness to a primal horror from our squalid makeshift bunker,
made from cinder blocks recovered from a moribund abattoir.
In that chamber undercover, I lay quiet—undiscovered,
silent as a child smothered—any noise, my saboteur.

Just as soon as it all started, asteroids passed by—then departed.
Odds of cataclysm rising ten percent moments before.
What I supposed in my surmising, finding it bitterly surprising,
was how welcomed the uprising was by those I now deplored.

On a fallen humankind, Apollyon's judgment I implored:

"Go, withdraw you cursed coward! Leave my seething soul untoward.
Leave a trail of stardust fading, fleeting from your feeble core.
Stay your true and righteous judgment—while the vile remain unpunished!
Fail to grant me just this one wish, made behind a collapsing door."
All our naive prayers soon pooled into a slick upon the floor.

As the stardust lost its shimmer, so my anger there too withered,
to an apathetic sadness saturating all I had adored.
Once, where I had burned with ire, now I searched for some desire—
something to ignite the pyre built on pretense I had stored.
Oh, how I yearned for fire to immolate the bastard horde.

Sifting through coarse ashen plaster, remnants of that grand disaster,
I realized life had passed me faster—faster than I'd felt before.
Never reaching a crescendo, ever nearing to my end though,
I surrendered, entrusting vengeance to a just and Sovereign Lord.
Now, as the starlit seas again recede, an old man greets the crimson shore.

ACCLAIMED

If ever I sought a critic's review—
my work yet unknown, except to a few—
the critique I would seek as utmost and salient,
would be my name followed by two words:
    "Is brilliant!"

For poetry, perhaps, a major award?
At last, recognition for some pairing of words!
In new ways, phrases appeal where they hadn't,
leading readers away to new worlds—
    "That's brilliant!"

For humility's sake, I'd report that I'm average,
lending critics their credence—affording them leverage.
Yet for a pleasant appraisal, there's no need for resilience.
I'd be pleased to retire on kind agreement:
    "So brilliant!"

www.ingramcontent.com/pod-product-compliance
Lightning Source LLC
Chambersburg PA
CBHW060420050426
42449CB00009B/2051